# MUSICIANS IN ACTION

# 50 Ready-to-Use Activities
# for Grades 3-9

# MUSICIANS IN ACTION

## 50 Ready-to-Use Activities for Grades 3–9

*Audrey J. Adair*

*Illustrated by Leah Solsrud*

**MUSIC CURRICULUM ACTIVITIES LIBRARY**

Parker Publishing Company, Inc.
West Nyack, N.Y.

© 1987 by

PARKER PUBLISHING COMPANY, INC.

West Nyack, N.Y.

**Library of Congress Cataloging-in-Publication Data**

Adair, Audrey J.
  Musicians in action.

  (Music curriculum activities library ; unit 7)
  1. School music—Instruction and study.   2. Music—
Vocational guidance.   I. Title.   II. Series: Adair,
Audrey J.,                    Music curriculum activities
library ; unit 7.
MT10.A14   1987   unit 7   372.8'7 s [372.8'7]   87-8833

ISBN 0-13-607144-9

Printed in the United States of America

# About the Author

Audrey J. Adair has taught music at all levels in the Houston, Texas, and Dade County, Florida, public schools. She has served as a music consultant, music specialist, general music instructor, choir director, and classroom teacher. In addition, she has written a series of musical programs for assemblies and holiday events, conducted music workshops, organized music programs for the community, established glee club organizations, and done specialization work with gifted and special needs students. Currently, she directs and coordinates children's choirs, performs as soloist with flute as well as voice, and composes sacred music.

Mrs. Adair received her B.A. in Music Education from St. Olaf College in Northfield, Minnesota, and has done graduate work at the University of Houston and Florida Atlantic University in Fort Lauderdale. She is also the author of *Ready-to-Use Music Activities Kit* (Parker Publishing Company), a resource containing over 200 reproducible worksheets to teach basic music skills and concepts.

# About the *Library*

The *Music Curriculum Activities Library* was developed for you, the busy classroom teacher or music specialist, to provide a variety of interesting, well-rounded, step-by-step activities ready for use in your music classroom. The *Library*'s seven carefully planned Units combine imagination, motivation, and student involvement to make learning as exciting as going on a field trip and as easy as listening to music.

The units of the *Music Curriculum Activities Library* are designed to be used separately or in conjunction with each other. Each Unit contains 50 *all new* ready-to-use music activity sheets that can be reproduced as many times as needed for use by individual students. These 350 illustrated, easy-to-read activities will turn even your most reluctant students into eager learners. Each Unit offers a wealth of information on the following topics:

Unit 1: *Basic Music Theory* develops an understanding of the basic elements of melody, rhythm, harmony, and dynamics.

Unit 2: *Reading and Writing Music* provides a source of reinforcement and instills confidence in the beginner performer through a wide range of note-reading and writing activities in the treble clef, bass clef, and in the clef of one's own instrument.

Unit 3: *Types of Musical Form and Composition* gives the student the foundation needed to enjoy worthwhile music by becoming acquainted with a wide variety of styles and representative works.

Unit 4: *Musical Instruments and the Voice* provides knowledge of and insight into the characteristic sounds of band, orchestra, folk instruments, and the voice.

Unit 5: *Great Composers and Their Music* familiarizes the student with some of the foremost composers of the past and present and their music; and cultivates an early taste for good music.

Unit 6: *Special Days Throughout the Year* offers the student well-illustrated, music-related activities that stimulate interest and discussion about music through holidays and special occasions for the entire school year.

Unit 7: *Musicians in Action* helps the student examine music as a pastime or for a career by exploring daily encounters with music and the skills, duties, environment, and requirements of a variety of careers in music.

# How to Use the *Library*

The activities in each Unit of the *Library* may be sequenced and developed in different ways. The general teacher may want to use one activity after the other, while the music specialist may prefer to use the activities in conjunction with the sequencing of the music curriculum. Teachers with special or individualized needs may select activities from various Units and use them over and over before actually introducing new material.

Let's take a closer look at how you can use the *Music Curriculum Activities Library* in your particular classroom situation:

... For THE MUSIC TEACHER who is accountable for teaching classes at many grade levels, there is a wide range of activities with varying degrees of difficulty. The activity sheets are ideal to strengthen and review skills and concepts suitable for the general music class.

... For THE NEW TEACHER STARTING A GENERAL MUSIC CLASS, these fun-filled activities will provide a well-balanced, concrete core program.

... For THE SPECIALIZED TEACHER who needs to set definite teaching goals, these activities offer a wealth of information about certain areas of music, such as career awareness, composers, and musical forms.

... For THE BAND AND CHOIR DIRECTOR, these activity sheets are a valuable resource to explore band, orchestra, and folk instruments, along with the singing voice.

... For THE PRIVATE MUSIC TEACHER who wants to sharpen and improve students' note reading skills, the *Library* offers ample homework assignments to give students the additional practice they need. There are many activity sheets using the clef of one's instrument and theory pages with illustrations of the keyboard.

... For THE MUSIC CONSULTANT using any one of the units, there are plenty of activities specifically correlated to the various areas of music providing reinforcement of learning. The activity sheets are suitable for class adoption in correlation with any music book series.

... For THE THEORY TEACHER, there are activities to show the students that music analysis is fun and easy.

... For THE TEACHER WHO NEEDS AN ADEQUATE MEANS OF EVALUATING STUDENT PROGRESS, there are fact-filled activities ideal for diagnostic purposes. A space is provided on each sheet for a score to be given.

. . . For THE CLASSROOM TEACHER with little or no musical background, the *Library* offers effective teaching with the flexibility of the seven units. All that has to be done is to decide on the music skill or concept to be taught and then duplicate the necessary number of copies. Even the answers can be duplicated for self-checking.

. . . For THE SUBSTITUTE TEACHER, these sheets are ideal for seatwork assignments because the directions are generally self-explanatory with minimal supervision required.

. . . For THE INSTRUCTOR OF GIFTED STUDENTS, the activities may be used for any type of independent, individualized instruction and learning centers. When used in an individualized fashion, the gifted student has an opportunity to pursue music learning at his or her own pace.

. . . For THE TEACHER OF SPECIAL EDUCATION, even the disadvantaged and remedial student can get in on the fun. Each concept or skill will be mastered as any lesson may be repeated or reinforced with another activity. Some of these activity sheets are designed to provide success for students who have difficulty in other subject areas.

. . . For the INDIVIDUAL who desires to broaden and expand his or her own knowledge and interest in music, each Unit provides 50 activities to help enjoy music.

The *Music Curriculum Activities Library* is ideally a teacher's program because a minimum of planning is required. A quick glance at the Contents in each Unit reveals the titles of all the activity sheets, the ability level necessary to use them, and the skills involved for each student. Little knowledge of music is generally needed to introduce the lessons, and extensive preparation is seldom necessary. You will, of course, want to read through the activity before presenting it to the class. In cases where you need to give information about the activity, two different approaches might be considered. (1) Use the activity as a basis for a guided discussion before completing the activity to achieve the desired results, or (2) Use the activity as a foundation for a lesson plan and then follow up by completing the activity. Either one of these approaches will enhance your own and your students' confidence and, by incorporating a listening or performing experience with this directed study, the students will have a well-rounded daily lesson.

All activity sheets throughout the *Library* have the same format. They are presented in an uncluttered, easy-to-read fashion, with self-explanatory directions. You need no extra materials or equipment, except for an occasional pair of scissors. The classroom or resource area should, however, contain a few reference books, such as song books or music series' books, encyclopedias, reference books about composers, a dictionary, music dictionary or glossary, and so on, so that while working on certain activities the student has easy access to resource books. Then, you simply need to duplicate the activity sheet as many times as needed and give a copy to each student. Even paper grading can be kept to a minimum by reproducing the answer key for self-checking.

The collection of activities includes practice in classifying, matching, listing, researching, naming, drawing, decoding, identifying, doing picture or crossword puzzles, anagrams, word searches, musical word squares, and much much more.

These materials may be used successfully with students in grades 3 and up. The activities and artwork are intentionally structured to appeal to a wide range of ages. For this reason, no grade-level references appear on the activity sheets so that you can use them in a variety of classroom settings, although suggested ability levels (beginner, intermediate, advanced) appear in the Contents.

The potential uses for the *Library* for any musical purpose (or even interdisciplinary study) are countless. Why? Because these activities allow you to instruct an entire class, a smaller group within the classroom, or individual students. While you are actively engaged in teaching one group of students, the activity sheets may be completed by another group. In any kind of classroom setting, even with the gifted music student or the remedial child, no student needs to sit idle. Now you will have more time for individual instruction.

The Units may be used in a comprehensive music skills program, in an enrichment program, or even in a remedial program. The *Library* is perfect for building a comprehensive musicianship program, improving basic music skills, teaching career awareness, building music vocabulary, exploring instruments, developing good taste in listening to music, appreciating different types of music, creating a positive learning environment, and providing growing confidence in the performer.

# What Each Unit Offers You

A quick examination of the **Contents** will reveal a well balanced curriculum. Included are the titles of all activities, the level of difficulty, and the skill involved. The exception to this is Unit 6, where the date and special day, rather than the skill, are listed with the title of each activity.

Each of the **50 reproducible activity sheets** generally presents a single idea, with a consistent format and easy-to-follow directions on how to do the activity, along with a sufficient amount of material to enable the student to become proficient through independent and self-directed work. Because each activity has but one single behavioral objective, mastery of each skill builds confidence that allows the learner to continue progressively toward a more complete understanding of the structure of music, appreciation of music, and its uses. The activity sheets are just the right length, too, designed to be completed within a class period.

The **Progress Chart** provides a uniform, objective method of determining what skills have been mastered. With the aid of this chart, you will be able to keep track of goals, set priorities, organize daily and weekly lesson plans, and track assignments. The Progress Chart lists each activity and skill involved, and has a space for individual names or classes to be recorded and checked when each activity and skill is complete. The Progress Chart is ideal for accurate record keeping. It provides a quick, sure method for you to determine each individual student's achievements or weaknesses.

Use the **Teacher's Guide** for practical guidance on how the particular Unit will work for you. An easy effective learning system, this guide provides background information and reveals new techniques for teaching the Unit.

Throughout the *Library*, each **Answer Key** is designed with a well-thought-out system for checking students' answers. While some activities are self-checking without the use of the Answer Key, other activities can easily be student corrected, too, by simply duplicating the answer page and cutting apart the answers by activity number.

**The Self-Improvement Chart** provides the student with a self-assessment system that links curriculum goals with individual goals. By means of an appraisal checklist, the chart gives the student and teacher alike the key to finding individual talent. It also measures accountability. Included in the chart are (1) a method for recording goals and acquired music skills; (2) a log for attendance at special music events; (3) a music and instrument check-out record; (4) a log for extra credit activities and music projects; (5) a record of special music recognition awards, incentive badges, Music Share-a-Grams, Return-a-Grams; and (6) a record of music progress.

These specific features of the chart will help you:

- Provide a uniform, objective method of determining rewards for students.
- Assess future curriculum needs by organizing long-term information on student performance.
- Foster understanding of why students did or did not qualify for additional merit.
- Motivate students by giving them feedback on ways for self-improvement.
- Assist students in making statements of their own desires and intentions for learning, and in checking progress toward their goals.

The **Music Share-a-Gram** is a personalized progress report addressed to the parent and created to show the unique qualities of the individual child. It allows you to pinpoint areas of success and tell parents what they need to know about their child. The Music Share-a-Gram evaluates twelve important abilities and personal traits with ratings from exceptional to unsatisfactory, which you might want to discuss with students to solicit their reaction. For example, you might use these ratings as a basis for selecting a student to attend the gifted program in music. This form is designed to be sent with or without the Return-a-Gram, and may be hand-delivered by the student or sent through the mail. For easy record keeping, make a copy of the Gram and attach it to the back of the Student Record Profile Chart.

The **Return-a-Gram** is designed to accompany the Music Share-a-Gram and is sent to the parent on special occasions. When a reply is not expected or necessary, simply detach the Return-a-Gram before sending the Share-a-Gram. This form encourages feedback from the parent and even allows the parent to arrange for a parent-teacher conference. Both Grams are printed on the same page and are self-explanatory—complete with a dotted line for the parent to detach, fill in, and return.

The **Student Record Profile Chart** is a guide for understanding and helping students, and offers a means of periodic evaluation. The chart is easy to use and provides all you need for accurate record keeping and measuring accountability for individual student progress throughout all seven units. It provides an accumulative skills profile for the student and represents an actual score of his or her written performance for each activity. Here is a workable form that you can immediately tailor to your own requirements for interpretation and use of scores. Included are clear instructions, with an example, to help you record your students' assessment on a day-to-day basis, to keep track of pupil progress, and to check learning patterns over a period of time. This chart allows you to spot the potential superior achiever along with the remedial individual. The chart coordinates all aspects of data ranging from the students' name, class, school, classroom teacher's name, semester, date, page number, actual grade, and attendance.

The **Word List** is presented as a reinforcement for building a music vocabulary. It emphasizes the use of dictionary skills; the students make a glossary of important words related to the particular unit. Its purpose is to encourage the use of vocabulary skills by helping develop an understanding of the music terms, concepts, and names found on the activity sheets. This vocabulary reference page is meant to be reproduced and used by the individual student throughout the units as a guide for spelling, word recognition, pronunciation, recording definitions, plus any other valuable information. Throughout six units of the *Library*, a cumulation of the words are presented on the Word List pages. (A Word List is not included in Unit 6.) With the help of this extensive vocabulary, when the student uses the words on both the activity page and the Word List, they will become embedded as part of his or her language.

Each Unit contains a wide-ranging collection of **Incentive Badges**. Use them to reward excellence, commend effort, for bonuses, prizes, behavior modification, or as reminders. These badges are designed to capture the interest and attention of the entire school. Several badges are designed with an open-ended format to provide maximum flexibility in meeting any special music teaching requirement.

Included in each Unit is a simple **Craft Project** that may be created by the entire class or by individual students. Each craft project is an integral part of the subject matter of that particular unit and will add a rich dimension to the activities. The materials necessary for the construction of the craft projects have been limited to those readily available in most classrooms and call for no special technical or artistic skills.

**PLUS** each Unit contains:

- Worked-out sample problems for students to use as a standard and model for their own work.

- Additional teaching suggestions in the Answer Key for getting the most out of certain activities.

- Extra staff paper for unlimited use, such as composing, ear training, improvising, or writing chords.

- Activities arranged in a sequential pattern.

# Resources for Teaching Music More Effectively

- Have a classroom dictionary available for reference.
- Have a glossary or music dictionary available for reference.
- Use only one activity sheet per class session.
- Distribute the Word List prior to the first activity sheet of the particular unit. Encourage students to underline familiar words on the list and write definitions or identifications on the back before instruction on the unit begins. Later, the students can compare their answers with those studied.
- Provide short-term goals for each class session and inform students in advance that awards will be given for the day. You'll see how their conduct improves, too.
- Encourage students to make or buy an inexpensive folder to store music activity sheets, craft projects, word lists, self-evaluation charts, and so on. Folders might be kept in the classroom when not in use and distributed at the beginning of each class period.
- Many of the activities are ideal for bulletin board display. If space is not available to display all students' work, rotate the exhibits.
- Encourage students to re-read creative writing pages for clarity and accuracy before copying the final form on the activity sheet. Proofreading for grammatical and spelling errors should be encouraged.
- For creative drawing activities, encourage students to sketch their initial ideas on another sheet of paper first, then draw the finished product on the activity sheet. It is not necessary to have any technical ability in drawing to experience the pleasure of these creative activities.
- Although you will probably want to work through parts of some activities with your students, and choose some activities for group projects, you will find that most lessons are designed to lead students to the correct answers with little or no teacher direction. Students can be directed occasionally to work through an activity with a partner to search out and correct specific errors.
- Self-corrections and self-checking make a much better impression on young learners than do red-penciled corrections by the classroom music teacher.
- On activities where answers will vary, encourage students to rate their own work on correctness, originality, completeness, carefulness, realism, and organization.

• Most activity pages will serve as a "teacher assistant" in developing specific skills or subject areas to study. The activities throughout the series are complete with learning objectives and are generally factual enough for the teacher to use as a basis for a daily lesson plan.

• The library research activities promote creativity instead of copying while students search out relevant data from a variety of sources, such as encyclopedias, dictionaries, reference books, autobiographies, and others. These activities are ideal for the individual student or groups of students working beyond the classroom environment.

• The following are practical guidelines in planning, organizing, and constructing the Craft Projects:

    . . . Acquaint yourself with any of the techniques that are new to you before you ask your students to undertake the project.

    . . . Decide on your project and assemble the materials before you begin.

    . . . Make a sample model for experience.

    . . . Use a flat surface for working.

    . . . Be sure the paper is cut exactly to measurements and that folds are straight.

    . . . Be available for consultation.

    . . . Provide guidance on what the next logical step is to encourage all students to finish their projects.

    . . . Use the finished craft projects as displays and points of interest for your school's open house.

• Many of the Incentive Badges found in each Unit are open-ended and can be made effective communication tools to meet your needs. Extra space is provided on these badges for additional written messages that might be used for any number of reasons. Be creative for your own special needs; load the copier with colored paper and print as many as you need for the semester or entire school year. Then simply use a paper cutter to separate the badges and sort them out alphabetically. Make an alphabetical index on file card dividers using these titles. Next, arrange them in an accessible file box or shoe box, depending on the size needed. Include a roll of tape to attach the badge to the recipient.

# Teacher's Guide to Unit 7

The purpose of *Musicians in Action* is to provide a supplementary music program for students by exploring music for enjoyment and music as a career. Unit 7 shows how music can affect people's daily lives in a positive way by reinforcing the concept that listening to music may be done for pleasure or enjoyed when performed as a hobby. This unit is also designed to broaden a student's understanding and appreciation of different music-related careers.

Unit 7 is divided into five sections. Four of the five sections use the technique of role-playing. This learning device assists in self-evaluation and provides feedback. Role-playing also helps students learn to respect and accept differences through sharing and discussing their lessons. With positive reinforcement by you and other students, role-playing will help develop self-esteem. An example of this is the activity "See Me at the Met" in which the student draws a picture of himself or herself singing at the Metropolitan Opera House. This activity might serve as an introduction to a special performance that the students will attend, or would be ideal as a follow-up to attending a concert or even watching a special music presentation on television. Just as positive verbal approval and interaction of praise might be encouraged while sharing finished activities, appropriate concert behavior such as smiling, nodding, and applauding must be encouraged.

Many of this unit's activities can be valuable resources for creative expression. Examples of this are "Make a Promotional Video" and "Review the Critic." Other activities, such as "Finish the Consumer's Guide" and "Check the Classified" are suitable for interdisciplinary study.

An integral part of music education and a concept stressed in Unit 7 is acquainting students with careers in music. If only a few class sessions are devoted to career awareness, divide the class into groups, with each group responsible for researching and reporting back to the others about a particular music career. A wide range of careers could then be explored to provide students with an overview in a short period of time. A quick glance at the Contents provides an accurate description of the music career (in parentheses) along with the title of the activity.

Whether students are interested in pursuing a career in music or not, they can benefit from learning how music influences their lives, and discovering how it can make performing and listening experiences more enjoyable and meaningful.

# Contents

| Activity Number/Title | Skill Involved | Level of Difficulty |
|---|---|---|
| **Role Playing in the World of Work** | | |
| 7-1 DELIVER THE EXPRESS MAIL | Drawing an item to match the job title | Beginner |
| 7-2 DISTRIBUTE THE MUSIC (Music Librarian) | Matching the name to the instrument | Beginner |
| 7-3 INTERVIEW THE CONDUCTOR (Conductor) | Matching interview questions with answers | Beginner |
| 7-4 THEY'RE REMEMBERED BY . . . (Historian) | Decoding names of famous composers and determining how they are remembered | Beginner |
| 7-5 WORK THE COMPUTER (Computer Programmer) | Answering general composition questions using a syllabic computer | Intermediate |
| **Role Playing Through Creative Drawing** | | |
| 7-6 BEST IN THE WORLD | Drawing an instrumentalist or vocalist performing a favorite type of music | Beginner |
| 7-7 SEE ME AT THE MET (Opera Star) | Drawing oneself on stage at the Metropolitan Opera House | Beginner |
| 7-8 CUSTOM MADE (Instrumentalist) | Drawing two musicians ready to perform for two different events | Beginner |
| 7-9 SKETCH A SCENE (Scene Designer) | Drawing a scene from a favorite musical | Beginner |
| 7-10 DESIGN YOUR SET (Set Designer) | Creating a set for a favorite production | Beginner |
| 7-11 GUESS WHO | Choosing a person for outstanding music achievement and illustrating the person | Beginner |
| 7-12 BE A STAGE MANAGER (Stage Manager) | Drawing items to be delivered to orchestra members | Beginner |

# Contents

| Activity Number/Title | Skill Involved | Level of Difficulty |
|---|---|---|
| 7-29 CHECK THE CLASSIFIED | Reading ads to decide where to call for certain music-related jobs | Beginner |
| 7-30 COMPOSER CROSSWORD | Using words from the puzzle to complete statements about composers | Beginner |
| 7-31 LEARNING ABOUT LYRICISTS AND ARRANGERS (Lyricist and Arranger) | Using letters from the keyboard to complete sentences about the lyricist and arranger | Beginner |
| 7-32 A TUNER'S CHOICE (Piano Tuner) | Completing sentences about the piano tuner using multiple choice | Intermediate |
| 7-33 RIGHT ON TARGET | Matching general music career-related questions with answers | Intermediate |
| 7-34 CHECK YOUR SPELLING (Music Librarian) | Using the dictionary to match music words with their definitions | Intermediate |
| 7-35 PUTTING THE PIECES TOGETHER | Matching jobs and descriptions relating to producing a musical | Intermediate |
| 7-36 CALL ON US | Listing people in the community to call for music-related questions | Intermediate |
| 7-37 COMPOSING A SONG (Composer) | Answering true/false statements about the composers | Intermediate |
| 7-38 BREAKING INTO POP (Pop Musician) | Matching questions with answers about becoming a pop musician | Intermediate |
| 7-39 EMPTY THE QUESTION BOX (Symphony Administrator) | Matching jobs in the symphony with their descriptions | Advanced |

**Role Playing Using Note-Reading Skills**

| | | |
|---|---|---|
| 7-40 WRITE A NEW SCHOOL SONG (Lyricist) | Writing lyrics for a new school song | Beginner |
| 7-41 TIGHT SQUEEZE (Transcriber) | Rewriting a song using better spacing than that in the example | Beginner |
| 7-42 TRANSCRIBE FOR BEETHOVEN (Transcriber) | Using dotted quarter notes listed to complete the theme for "Eroica" | Beginner |
| 7-43 MAKE A PROMOTIONAL VIDEO (Songwriter) | Creating lyrics to the tune of Mozart's 40th and drawing four scenes for a football promo | Intermediate |
| 7-44 MAKE A DEMO TAPE (Orchestrator) | Creating two percussion scores to accompany the song "Bingo" | Intermediate |

| Activity Number/Title | Skill Involved | Level of Difficulty |
|---|---|---|
| 7–45 PROGRAM THE COMPUTER (Computer Programmer) | Drawing quarter notes in the key of F Major to complete a tune by Schumann | Intermediate |
| 7–46 BE AN ORCHESTRATOR (Orchestrator) | Composing an original rhythmic composition in ABA form | Intermediate |
| 7–47 WHAT'S THE TITLE? (Music Historian) | Recognizing beginning lines of Stephen Foster songs by listening to the melodies | Intermediate |
| 7–48 WRITE A JINGLE (Songwriter) | Composing a melody and lyrics for a television commercial | Intermediate and Advanced |
| 7–49 SWEET DREAMS (Composer) | Writing a verse for a lullaby and composing a melody to accompany it | Intermediate and Advanced |
| 7–50 TRANSPOSE IT FOR THE CLARINET (Arranger) | Transposing a simple tune from the Key of B-flat Major to C Major | Intermediate and Advanced |

# Activities for
# ROLE PLAYING IN THE WORLD OF WORK

# DELIVER THE EXPRESS MAIL                                           7–1

You are the delivery person for a shipment of overnight mail. Your job is to deliver this list of items to the following people's places of work. Write the letter name of the item on the line that matches the job title, and draw the item at the appropriate place in the picture.

a.  podium
b.  bow
c.  staff paper

d.  chair
e.  Beethoven's piano sonatas
f.  A new book on the life of Aaron Copland

____ 1.  Symphony member     ____ 2.  Symphony member     ____ 3.  Conductor

____ 4.  Music librarian     ____ 5.  Pianist     ____ 6.  Composer

# DISTRIBUTE THE MUSIC                         7–2

The music librarian has left for the post office to pick up a new orchestral score. Rehearsal is about to begin. You have volunteered to pass out the music. To help you do this job, write the name of the instrument in the music stand by its matching picture. The names of the instruments pictured below are listed alphabetically.

cello
clarinet
flute
French horn
harp
kettledrums
viola
violin

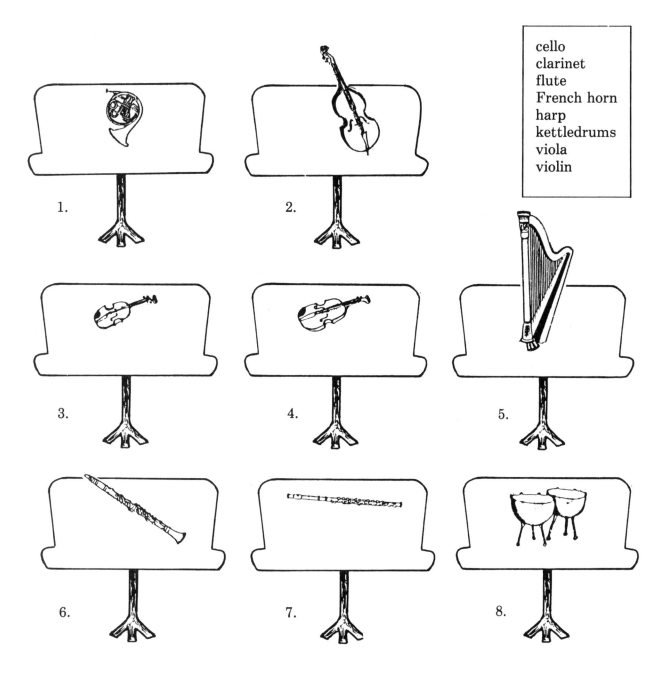

1.

2.

3.

4.

5.

6.

7.

8.

## INTERVIEW THE CONDUCTOR

Imagine that you are interviewing a conductor for your community orchestra. Here are the questions you will be asking. Find the conductor's answers on the bottom half of the page and write the identifying letter after the question.

1. What type of ensemble experience have you had? ____

2. What type of conducting experience have you had? ____

3. What do you do to broaden your exposure to different types of performances? ____

4. What leadership qualities do you have that make you a successful conductor? ____

5. Why do you think you'd be right for the job? ____

Draw the Conductor

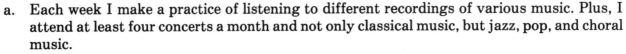

a. Each week I make a practice of listening to different recordings of various music. Plus, I attend at least four concerts a month and not only classical music, but jazz, pop, and choral music.

b. As you probably know, I'm a professor in music at your local university. With my broad musical background, my leadership abilities, and my interest in people, I feel I could be a real asset to your organization.

c. I've played violin with a youth orchestra, played in my high school orchestra, and college orchestra. During the summers I've also played flute with a jazz band.

d. While in college I participated in both choral and instrumental conducting courses. During that time I also gained experience conducting a choral ensemble and string ensemble.

e. My experience in fund-raisers has proven my leadership qualities. As you know I've had a great deal of conducting experience. When I had more time I organized a volunteer program at the hospital.

Name _____

Score _____

Date _____

Class _____

## THEY'RE REMEMBERED BY ...

A music historian has made a listing of how some famous composers are remembered. Figure out the secret code to name the composers.

1. _____ is remembered for his fugues, cantatas, and
   JOH ANN ASE BAS TIA NAB ACH A   chorale preludes.

2. _____ is remembered for his operas and his
   GEO RGE AFR EDE RIC KAH AND ELA   oratorios.

3. _____ is remembered for his nine symphonies, over-
   LUD WIG AVA NAB EET HOV ENA   tures, concertos, thirty-two piano sonatas, and
   much more.

4. _____ is remembered for being the only one of the world's great
   FRE DER ICA CHO PIN A   composers who made piano music his specialty.

5. _____ is remembered as the "father" of impressionism in music.
   CLA UDE ADE BUS SYA

6. _____ is remembered as the "father" of the symphony, sonata, and
   JOS EPH AHA YDN A   string quartet.

7. _____ is remembered as a child prodigy and
   WOL FGA NGA AMA DEU SAM OZA RTA   musical genius.

8. _____ is remembered for changing the destiny of opera single-
   RIC HAR DAW AGN ERA   handedly.

# WORK THE COMPUTER

Fill in the answers to the clues, using all the syllables in the Syllabic Computer. The number of syllables that will be used in each answer is shown in parentheses. The blank spaces indicate the number of letters needed in each answer word. Use each syllable only once.

1.  A screech produced when a microphone pickup is too close to its speaker.

    (2) _ _ _ _ _ _ _ _

2.  Changing music from one key to another

    (4) _ _ _ _ _ _ _ _ _ _ _ _

3.  An instrument for playing records.

    (3) _ _ _ _ _ _ _ _ _ _

4.  To write a piece in a different key

    (2) _ _ _ _ _ _ _ _

5.  Written music

    (3) _ _ _ _ _ _ _ _

6.  A type of country music for string instruments

    (2) _ _ _ _ _ _ _ _ _

7.  A composition for four players

    (2) _ _ _ _ _ _ _

8.  Refrain of a song

    (2) _ _ _ _ _ _

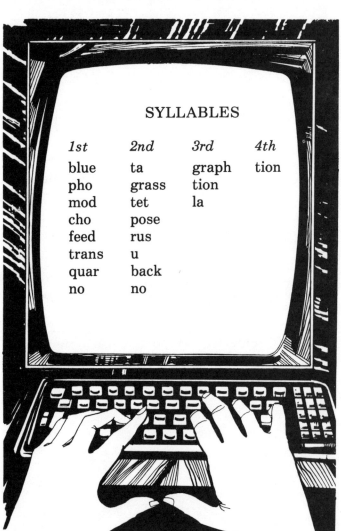

SYLLABLES

| 1st | 2nd | 3rd | 4th |
|------|------|------|------|
| blue | ta | graph | tion |
| pho | grass | tion | |
| mod | tet | la | |
| cho | pose | | |
| feed | rus | | |
| trans | u | | |
| quar | back | | |
| no | no | | |

# Activities for
# ROLE PLAYING THROUGH CREATIVE DRAWING

## BEST IN THE WORLD                                         7–6

Use the space below to draw a picture of instrumentalists
or vocalists performing your favorite type of music.

My most favorite type of music in the whole world is:

_____

Name _____     Score _____

Date _____     Class _____

## SEE ME AT THE MET

Imagine that you are singing a leading role with the Metropolitan Opera Company. Draw yourself on stage at the Metropolitan Opera House.

## CUSTOM MADE                                     7–8

Use the frame to the right to draw a musician ready to perform with the Boston Pops Symphony Orchestra. Include everything he or she will need for the concert, such as appropriate dress, an orchestral instrument, music, a music stand, and a chair.

Use this frame to the right to draw an instrumentalist playing with your favorite marching band in the Macy's Thanksgiving Day parade. Include everything he or she will need for the parade, such as an appropriate uniform, instrument, etc.

Name _____  Score _____

Date _____  Class _____

## SKETCH A SCENE                    7–9

Draw a scene from your favorite musical.

Name of musical _____  Composer _____

# DESIGN YOUR SET                                      7–10

Create a set for your favorite production. It could be from a musical, an operetta, or an opera. Sketch your finished plans on the stage below.

Name of production _____ Composer _____

## GUESS WHO                                     7–11

Imagine that you have been delegated to choose a person from your class for outstanding achievement in music. Pretend that this person will be presented with a trophy at an all-school assembly. Write the name of the person you selected on the back of this page. In the frame below draw a picture of this person receiving the trophy from your principal.

## BE A STAGE MANAGER                                    7–12

It's almost time for the concert to begin. These four orchestra members cannot perform with the symphony unless you arrange for them to get the following items: music stand, chair, reed and bow. Draw a picture of the item by the person to whom it will be delivered.

VIOLA PLAYER

1.

DOUBLE BASS          PLAYER

2.

FLUTIST

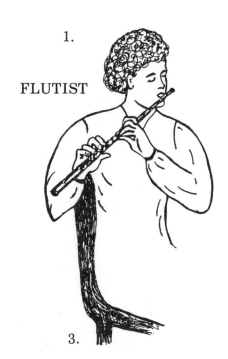

3.

OBOIST

4.

# DELIVER THE GOODS

7–13

Each of these people placed an order at the "We've Got It Music Store." You are in charge of the delivery. Finish drawing these pictures to show the people using the items you delivered.

Goods to be delivered: strings, baton, bugle, staff paper

# Activities for
# ROLE PLAYING THROUGH CREATIVE WRITING

Name _____    Score _____

Date _____    Class _____

## LET'S GO SHOPPING                                    7–14

Choose one item you would like to buy from this store. Tell why you've selected it, how you will use it, and name a career related to it.

| | | | |
|---|---|---|---|
| ELECTRIC ORGAN | VIOLA | PIANO | GUITAR |
| BELLS | DRUMS | STAFF PAPER | RECORDING EQUIPMENT |

1. Name of item: _____

2. Why I want it: _____

   _____

3. How I will use it: _____

   _____

4. Related career: _____

   _____

## PRETEND YOU ARE THE MUSIC THERAPIST          7–15

You have been asked to go to your local hospital and work with the children in the physical dis-
abilities unit. The children you are assigned have a special problem with eye–hand coordina-
tion. Your job is to use music to help their condition. What will you do? Describe your teaching
method for a simple music lesson with these children using the following guides.

OBJECTIVE: _____

_____

MATERIALS NEEDED: _____

_____

PROCEDURE: _____

_____

_____

_____

_____

_____

_____

_____

_____

_____

_____

_____

## BE A BIGWIG

7–16

First fold the bottom portion of
this page back. Then pretend you
are a bigwig from the music industry visiting the school to provide some guidance to aspiring
young musicians. The four high school students you will read about below all have clearly
defined goals and all want to become involved in a music-related field. Write your advice to
each student in the space provided. When you are finished, compare your advice to the
answers printed at the bottom of the page.

1. After Ryan graduates from college with a music major, he wants to make use of his musical
   education. He plans to play in an orchestra. What other work could he do to supplement his
   income?

   _____

   _____

   _____

2. Gillian wants to play in a symphony someday. She is a sophomore in high school. How can
   she get ensemble experience before entering college?

   _____

   _____

   _____

3. Jesse wants to become a professional musician. He is teaching himself to play the guitar.
   Should he continue on this course?

   _____

   _____

   _____

4. Allie is interested in orchestra management. How can she prepare for a career in this field?

   _____

   _____

   _____

------------------------------ fold back ------------------------------

1. Become a music teacher; give private lessons; become a church musician; audition for other
   music jobs around town.
2. Join a youth orchestra; attend summer music camp; organize an ensemble group to perform
   at local P.T.A. meetings and community functions.
3. No, he will need years of private lessons to study his instrument.
4. Do volunteer work with a professional symphony orchestra, and combine music studies in
   college with business studies.

Name _____    Score _____

Date _____    Class _____

# QUESTIONNAIRE ABOUT THE CHURCH MUSICIAN    7-17

Musicians play important roles in churches and synagogues. See
how many of these questions you can answer about the church
musician.

1. What are the responsibilities of the church organist?

_____

_____

_____

2. What are the responsibilities of the choir director?

_____

_____

_____

3. What are the different types of choirs one might find in a church?

_____

_____

_____

4. Explain what a handbell choir is.

_____

_____

_____

5. What are the responsibilities of the "Minister of Music?"

_____

_____

_____

_____

## ASK THE RECRUITER

Pretend that you are interested in a music career with the Armed Forces (Army, Navy, Air Force, or Marine Corps). A recruiter has come to your school and you had an opportunity to ask questions. Here are the answers. What were your questions? Write a question to match each answer.

© 1987 by Parker Publishing Company, Inc.

### QUESTION

### ANSWER

1. _____
   _____
   _____

"You need a high school diploma, proficiency on an instrument, and basic knowledge of music theory."

2. _____
   _____
   _____

"There are unlimited career opportunities in music. There's a need for instrumentalists, vocalists, accompanists, teachers, transcribers, recording technicians, instrument repairing personnel, and more."

3. _____
   _____
   _____

"Gain as much practical experience as you can in any kind of band or instrumental group or vocal ensemble through your school or community."

4. _____
   _____
   _____

"Auditions are held prior to enlistment."

5. _____
   _____
   _____

"Not necessarily. The training you'll have will be excellent preparation for a music career even if you later leave the Armed Forces."

6. _____
   _____
   _____

"The pay scale is competitive with civilian wages. There's medical care, retirement pay, and privileges at the commissary and post exchange."

Name _____     Score _____

Date _____     Class _____

# REVIEW THE CRITIC

Find a review from a music event in the newspaper. Attach it to the back of this page and answer the following questions about the review.

Name of music critic: _____

Name of music event: _____

When was the event held? _____

Where was the event held? _____

What did the music critic like most about the performance?

_____

_____

_____

_____

What did the music critic like least about the performance?

_____

_____

_____

_____

_____

## PLAN AHEAD

Imagine that you are a music intern for one class period. You will be teaching one music class of your choice. Plan the lesson using the "Teacher's Plan Book" below.

### TEACHER'S PLAN BOOK

Teacher's name _____ Date _____

Teaching objective: _____

_____

_____

Materials needed: _____

_____

Procedure: _____

_____

_____

_____

_____

_____

Evaluation: _____

_____

_____

## BE A PERSONNEL DIRECTOR                    7–21

Pretend that you are a personnel director for a company in the music industry. Write a job description for a position that is available. You decide the specific job. It could be in the recording business, television, or some other area. Include the responsibilities, the hours, the fringe benefits, and the salary.

POSITION AVAILABLE: _____

JOB DESCRIPTION:

_____

_____

_____

_____

_____

_____

_____

_____

_____

_____

_____

_____

_____

_____

_____

_____

_____

# WRITE A RÉSUMÉ

7-22

Pretend that you are seeking employment in the field of music. You decide what the job will be. Use the form below to complete a résumé to bring with you on your interview.

NAME: _____

ADDRESS: _____

TELEPHONE: _____

JOB OBJECTIVE: _____

_____

EXPERIENCE: _____

_____

_____

_____

_____

_____

EDUCATION: _____

_____

_____

_____

_____

SPECIAL SKILLS: _____

_____

_____

_____

REFERENCES: _____

_____

_____

# GET THE JOB

7-23

Pretend that you are applying for a job in the music profession. Write a letter of application in response to an ad you read in the newspaper. Be sure your letter attracts the reader's attention, arouses interest, and will get a response. State some brief facts about yourself—your job experience, your education, some personal facts. Tell why you want the job and what you can do to be an asset to your employer's company.

# Activities for
# EXPLORING MUSIC-RELATED JOBS
# THROUGH PROBLEM-SOLVING EXPERIENCES

## TOOLS OF THE TRADE                                      7-24

Match the tool with the job title by writing the name of the tool on the blank.

1. _____ recording artist

2. _____ violinist

3. _____ drummer

4. _____ conductor

5. _____ composer

6. _____ piano tuner

7. _____ guitarist

8. _____ trumpet player

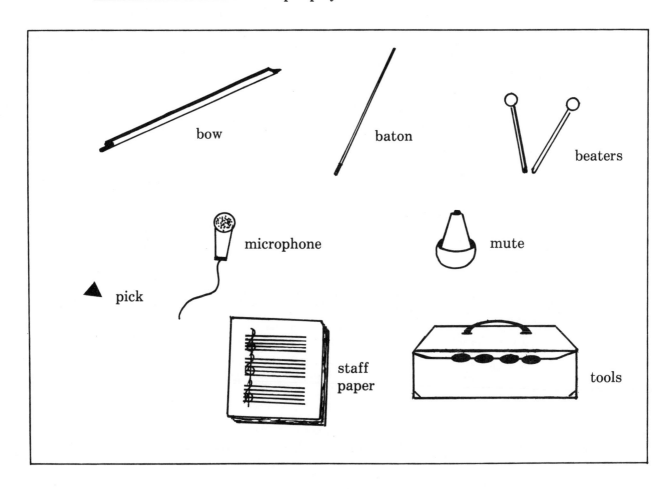

Name _____     Score _____

Date _____     Class _____

## A VISIT WITH THE PRIVATE MUSIC TEACHER     7–25

This story about the private music teacher has several words that are missing letters. Choose the missing letters from the C Major Scale to finish the words.

C   D   E   F   G   A   B   C

A private music teacher can have a very flexible (1) s __ h __ __ ul __ . Teaching can be a part-time or a full-time (2) jo __ . The private teacher is the boss and can plan his or her own schedule. Private teachers may work out of their homes, travel to their students' homes, work out of a music store, or use a music (3) stu __ io. The full-time private teacher has a busy schedule working after school and (4) w __ __ k __ n __ s.

The most popular instrument for private lessons is the (5) pi __ no. Two other instruments in demand that require a private teacher are the guitar and the (6) or __ __ n. Children as young as age three can now take private instruction (7) pl __ ying violin according to the Suzuki method.

To be a successful private music teacher, one should be able to perform better than his or her (8) __ __ st pupil. Besides being an outstanding musician, the private instructor must be a good (9) t __ __ __ h __ r. A private teacher should have enthusiasm and patience. A good teacher always seeks ways to (1) improv __ his or her skills.

## CLASSIFY THE STATIONS

7–26

Listen to at least two radio stations in your area to decide what type of music each plays. Classify the stations according to the music played. Suggested classifications are:

> public radio, top 40, classical, gospel, country, rhythm
> and blues, easy listening, contemporary, Latin, religious,
> big band, soul, oldies, middle-of-the-road, and jazz

Use the space below to record the following information on the chart. An example is given. You may double-check your answers with your local newspaper.

| Names of AM and/or FM radio stations in your area | What type of music does each station play? | What are the numbers on your dial? |
|---|---|---|
| WTMI (FM) | Classical | 93.1 |
|  |  |  |

# WHOM SHOULD I CONTACT?

7-27

Use the backwards answers to find the occupations of persons you would contact for the following jobs. Write your answers on the space provided.

1. You need someone to sing the national anthem for your next football game.

   _____
   tsilacov

2. You are looking for someone who is good at sight reading to play when you hold auditions for the choir.

   _____
   tsinapmocca

3. You have started a rock group and you need someone to take care of the publicity and get in touch with the "right" people.

   _____
   cilbup snoitaler rotcerid

4. You have just finished writing a television show and you are looking for someone to write a musical score to go with the show.

   _____
   resopmoc

5. Your friends have asked you to play guitar with their group. You are looking for someone to help you learn some songs in eight weeks.

   _____
   etavirp rehcaet

6. You have the melody, but you need individual parts for each member of your orchestra to play.

   _____
   regnarra

7. Your school is putting on a music festival. It's one of a kind and you would like someone from the local newspaper to give it some coverage.

   _____
   rotide

8. Your grades in music class need improvement and your parent is about to make a phone call to find out how you can do better.

   _____
   cisum rehcaet

## FINISH THE CONSUMER GUIDE                    7-28

As a consumer, where in your town would you purchase the goods or services on this list? Write your answers on the blanks. Here are some possibilities:

audio-visual store - book store - department store - electronics store - instrumental teacher - music store - record and tape store - video center - videotape store -vocal teacher

# CONSUMER GUIDE

1. guitar pick _____

2. "top ten" record _____

3. synthesizer _____

4. videotape _____

5. vocal lessons _____

6. instrumental lessons_____

7. pitch pipe _____

8. music dictionary _____

9. staff paper _____

10. gospel recording _____

11. book on the life of Mozart_____

12. piano _____

Name _____          Score _____

Date _____          Class _____

## CHECK THE CLASSIFIED                                    7–29

Read through the ads below. Then decide what number(s) you would call if you wanted:

1. To be singing with a jazz group _____

2. To be a church organist _____

3. To buy a music store _____

4. To take piano lessons _____

5. To audition for the symphony _____

6. Your group to play for concerts _____

7. To teach music in elementary school _____

8. A job as a drummer _____

# CLASSIFIED ADVERTISING

KEYBOARD PLAYER with lead vocal ability wanted for steady group. Call Greg after 4:30 pm 722-2801

Wanted 6-piece group to play top-40 soul and golden oldies. To play behind nationally known singer. For interview call 731-2828

TUTORING in music theory by certified music teacher. Immediate opening. Ask for J.R. 499-2834

BANDS WANTED for 1-nighters and concerts. 823-4568

CHURCH ORGANIST for local church. Call Mrs. Pastuer 8–4, wkdys 491-2390

MUSICIANS wanted for band. Sax, flute guitar. Call Bob after 6 pm 348-7682

EXPERIENCED TRIO for weddings, dances. Before 7 pm Mr. Walz 564-3890

ONE-MAN BAND for local club. Organ-accordion-electric piano. Dining and dancing. 782-4457

EXPERIENCED DRUMMER for top group 566-9781

MUSIC TEACHER for K–8 private school. Call between 8–3. 233-9457

PRIVATE VOCAL LESSONS in your own home Reasonable rates. 761-9823

PIANO AND ORGAN LESSONS. All ages. Private studio in NW area. 431-2806

MUSIC INSTRUCTION by local symphony member. Specializing in strings. Call 320-4938. Ask for Marg.

PARTNER for retail music store. Fantastic opportunity for hard working person. Minimum required $40,000 with terms. Sheet music knowledge helpful. 675-9723

RECORD SHOP. Good terms and lease. 339-2121

LEAD SINGER for jazz group. Must be able to travel. For audition call 766-4555

AUDITIONS for community symphony. Call Mr. Judge for appointment. 492-3660

## COMPOSER CROSSWORD                    7–30

The following statements are all about composers. Find the missing word in the puzzle and match it with the statement by writing it on the blank.

1.  Symphonic composers need to be familiar with all the instruments of the

    _____.

2.  A beginning composer or lyricist has difficulty supporting himself or her-

    self by writing _____.

3.  A composer needs to copyright his or her work before presenting it to a

    _____.

4.  The percentage of popular song writers that ever become successful

    is _____.

5.  Before 1960 a great song was usually

    written by a composer or _____.

6.  _____ was a great German composer and organist.

7.  Today, many of the composers who write popular music are also performing

    _____.

8.  An American symphonic composer is Aaron _____.

9.  One of the biggest problems for a symphonic composer is to find an orchestra that

    will play his or her new _____.

10. An understanding of music theory is necessary to become a _____.

11. A song for a single voice, as in opera, is called an _____.

12.–13. _____ is a term used for the words of a _____.

Name _____    Score _____

Date _____    Class _____

## LEARNING ABOUT LYRICISTS AND ARRANGERS          7–31

Each of these statements about the lyricists and arranger has a word that is missing one or more letters. Read the sentence and complete the word by using any of the letters from the keyboard at the bottom of the page.

1.  The lyricist writes the wor __ s to the song.

2.  A basic principle of writing songs is to keep the lyrics simpl __ .

3.  The lyri __ s are the words of the song.

4.  When writing lyrics, every word __ ounts.

5.  One item you would likely see on the desk of a lyricist is a rhyming __ i __ tion __ ry.

6.  An arranger may just add fresh material to a son __ .

7.  It is not necessary to r __ __ __ and write music to make an arrangement for a small rock group.

8.  The four basic elements to consider when arranging a piece of music are: the form, h __ rmony, rhythm, and melody.

9.  The most important part of arranging a piece of music is the m __ lo __ y.

10. When arranging a song for a string quartet, the arranger must use the treble clef, the C clef, and the bass __ l __ __ .

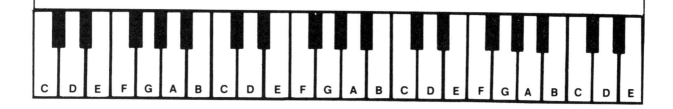

Name _____          Score _____

Date _____          Class _____

## A TUNER'S CHOICE                                          7-32

Test your knowledge of piano tuning by finding the correct conclusion to each sentence. Write the word in the blank.

1.  To be a piano tuner, you must also be a _____.
    a.  man                  b.  technician              c.  vocalist

2.  Piano tuners are generally _____.
    a.  independent          b.  wealthy                 c.  union members

3.  Piano tuners find that most of the pianos are located in _____.
    a.  homes                b.  churches                c.  schools

4.  A piano tuner regulates the mechanisms on a piano to provide the best possible intonation

    and top _____.
    a.  performance          b.  value                   c.  drawer

5.  The piano tuner will replace or repair any broken _____.
    a.  song books           b.  ailments                c.  parts

6.  The piano tuner must train his or her ear to hear the interferences, otherwise known as

    _____.
    a.  sound pulses         b.  beats                   c.  strings

7.  To manipulate the tuning lever, the piano tuner must coordinate the hand with the

    _____.
    a.  brain                b.  key                     c.  ear

8.  The piano tuner has special tools to regulate the piano action and _____.
    a.  temperament          b.  felts                   c.  keys

9.  Some institutions and music stores have full-time piano tuners known as

    _____.
    a.  sales people         b.  employees               c.  management

10. Tuning a piano is _____.
    a.  an acquired skill    b.  a musical talent        c.  difficult

# RIGHT ON TARGET

To be "right on target," write the correct letter on the numbered blank that answers the question.

1. ____ Why does a concert manager play an important role for a new performer?

2. ____ Why must an accompanist be able to transpose the music into a different key without advance notice?

3. ____ What reason is there for not hearing more about choral conductors?

4. ____ What might be the highest point of success for a star?

5. ____ Does a conductor need to be a master of several different instruments?

6. ____ If you are interested in becoming a solo performer, what can you do to gain experience?

7. ____ Does a solo performer need to be well educated?

8. ____ What do Juilliard and Eastman have in common?

9. ____ Where might an outstanding young musician go for a summer program centered on music?

10. ____ If you plan to be a performer, when should you start planning for it?

(M) Yes, he or she must be a complete musician to assist an orchestra.

(L) To the National Music Camp at Interlochen, Michigan.

(I) Right now.

(s) There are very few professional choirs throughout the country.

(o) They are schools of music.

(c) He or she arranges for ways to get the performer's name in front of the public.

(i) If, for example, a song is too high for a vocalist, he or she might request to perform the song in a different key.

(u) Performing at the Metropolitan Opera House in New York City.

(e) Find opportunities to perform in front of people on the stage, at school, home, community organizations, or at church.

(v) Yes, he or she must have knowledge of the history of development and know the musical style of the composer.

# CHECK YOUR SPELLING

Imagine that you are the music librarian, and you have planned a dictionary lesson for your students. Finish your plan by making an answer key so that the students can check their own work. First, circle each music word in the pairs below. Then, match that music word with its definition by writing the correct letter in the box.

| | | | |
|---|---|---|---|
| ☐ | 1. heir/air | a. | A unit of time |
| ☐ | 2. aria/area | b. | The number of beats in a measure |
| ☐ | 3. bass/base | c. | Tune, melody |
| ☐ | 4. beet/beat | d. | A number of movements in various dance forms |
| ☐ | 5. choir/quire | e. | An ancient stringed instrument |
| ☐ | 6. chorus/coarse | f. | The lowest part in a music composition |
| ☐ | 7. time/thyme | g. | A thin strip of cane |
| ☐ | 8. liar/lyre | h. | A lively rustic dance |
| ☐ | 9. pedal/petal | i. | An air, a song sung by a single voice |
| ☐ | 10. read/reed | j. | A group of singers; the refrain of a song |
| ☐ | 11. real/reel | k. | A mechanism controlled by the foot |
| ☐ | 12. sweet/suite | l. | A group of singers |

# PUTTING THE PIECES TOGETHER                    7–35

Complete this puzzle by matching the jobs involved in producing a musical with their descriptions listed below. Write the name of the job on the blanks using only one letter on each space. Then write the letter from the job list on the appropriate puzzle piece, being sure it matches the number of the job description. Your answers reading across will spell out a sentence.

**LIST OF JOBS**

O.  actor
R.  choreographer
U.  composer
F.  conductor
B.  critic
H.  investor
N.  lyricist
T.  manager, producer
E.  press agent
O.  set designer
J.  stage manager
R.  writer

**JOB DESCRIPTIONS**

1.  Puts the story down on paper: ___ ___ ___ ___ ___ ___

2.  Writes the music: ___ ___ ___ ___ ___ ___ ___ ___

3.  Writes the verse or poetry to set to music: ___ ___ ___ ___ ___ ___ ___ ___

4.  Directs the orchestra: ___ ___ ___ ___ ___ ___ ___ ___ ___

5.  Designs the set: ___ ___ ___  ___ ___ ___ ___ ___ ___ ___ ___

6.  Plans the dance steps: ___ ___ ___ ___ ___ ___ ___ ___ ___ ___ ___ ___ ___

7.  Has general charge of the production: ___ ___ ___ ___ ___ ___ ___ ___    OR

    ___ ___ ___ ___ ___ ___ ___ ___

8.  Has substantial money backing to invest in musical:

    ___ ___ ___ ___ ___ ___ ___ ___

9.  Promotes the musical: ___ ___ ___ ___ ___ ___  ___ ___ ___ ___ ___

10.  In charge of set properties: ___ ___ ___ ___ ___ ___  ___ ___ ___ ___ ___ ___ ___

11.  Acts on the stage: ___ ___ ___ ___ ___

12.  Reviews the musical for the media: ___ ___ ___ ___ ___ ___

Name _____

Date _____

Score _____

Class _____

## CALL ON US

What person (or business) in your community would you call for help in the following areas? Complete the chart with the name of the person or business, the type of business, and telephone number.

| PROBLEM | NAME OF PERSON OR BUSINESS | TYPE OF BUSINESS | TELEPHONE NUMBER |
|---|---|---|---|
| 1. The reed on your clarinet is broken and you need a new one. | | | |
| 2. Your piano needs tuning. | | | |
| 3. You want to know what time your PBS station airs the "Boston Pops." | | | |
| 4. You want to know the price of a new guitar. | | | |
| 5. You want to purchase tickets for the symphony that'll be performing in your area. | | | |
| 6. You want to begin organ lessons. | | | |
| 7. You want the most current videotape. | | | |
| 8. You want to know what your high school band is playing for its next concert. | | | |
| 9. You want the name of the editor who covers musical events for the local newspaper. | | | |
| 10. You'd like to talk to the P.T.A. or P.T.O. president about performing for an upcoming meeting. | | | |

Name _____    Score _____

Date _____    Class _____

# COMPOSING A SONG    7-37

The following statements about composing are either true or false. Circle T if the statement is true, or circle F if the statement is false. Then write the correction under each false statement.

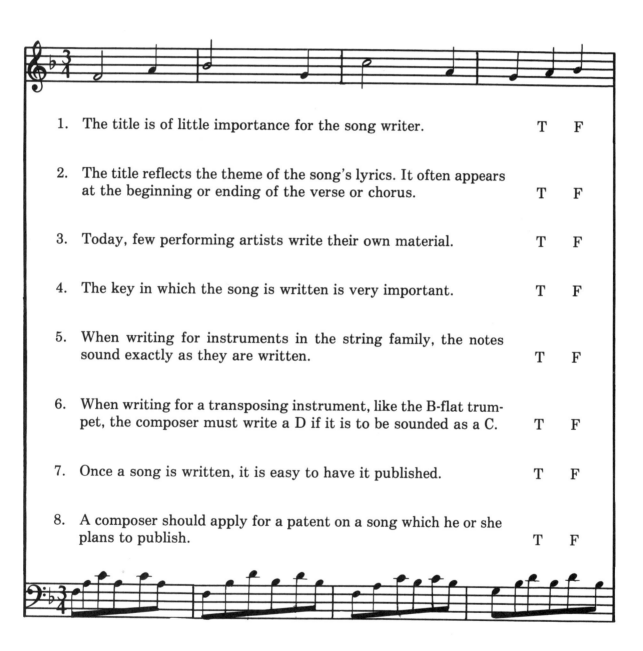

1.  The title is of little importance for the song writer.                              T       F

2.  The title reflects the theme of the song's lyrics. It often appears
    at the beginning or ending of the verse or chorus.                                  T       F

3.  Today, few performing artists write their own material.                             T       F

4.  The key in which the song is written is very important.                             T       F

5.  When writing for instruments in the string family, the notes
    sound exactly as they are written.                                                  T       F

6.  When writing for a transposing instrument, like the B-flat trum-
    pet, the composer must write a D if it is to be sounded as a C.                      T       F

7.  Once a song is written, it is easy to have it published.                            T       F

8.  A composer should apply for a patent on a song which he or she
    plans to publish.                                                                   T       F

## BREAKING INTO POP

7–38

These questions and answers about becoming a pop musician are all mixed up. Read through all the questions and answers to figure out what question goes with what answer. Write the identifying letter of the answer after the correct question. Then, check your answers by using the word code at the bottom of the page to spell a word.

1. Why is classical training important to the pop musician? ____

2. Why is knowing other musicians important if you want to be a performer? ____

3. What preparation may help you cut down on stage fright when appearing before the public? ____

4. How can you learn your favorite artists' techniques? ____

5. How can you participate in your community while you're still in school? ____

6. Why is a college degree in music helpful for a performer? ____

7. Why should you practice? ____

8. What is just as important as technical skills for a musician? ____

a. To be at your peak performance level, you must practice regularly.

b. Play for service clubs, join a community orchestra, perform at P.T.A. meetings, start your own group, and so on.

c. That's the only way you can be recommended and break into the music field.

d. Training in theory, form, and composition will broaden your musical background.

e. Individual style; it makes a performer different from someone else.

f. Play along with their recordings and watch videotapes.

g. To build a performing repertoire, you need advanced music theory and instrumental techniques offered in college.

h. Play for friends and family; much practice, in general.

------------------------------------------------------------

Now write the number that matches the first letter in each pair:

a = s ____     c = o ____     e = t ____     g = i ____

b = l ____     d = v ____     f = a ____     h = c ____

Now write the code letters in order from 1–8

$\overline{\quad}$ $\overline{\quad}$ $\overline{\quad}$ $\overline{\quad}$ $\overline{\quad}$ $\overline{\quad}$ $\overline{\quad}$ $\overline{\quad}$
  1    2    3    4    5    6    7    8

Name _____    Score _____

Date _____    Class _____

## EMPTY THE QUESTION BOX                                    7–39

A group of school children have just come back from a field trip touring the symphony hall. They put all their questions in this box and you are to answer them. To do this, write the question number at the bottom of the page in the blank by the matching job title.

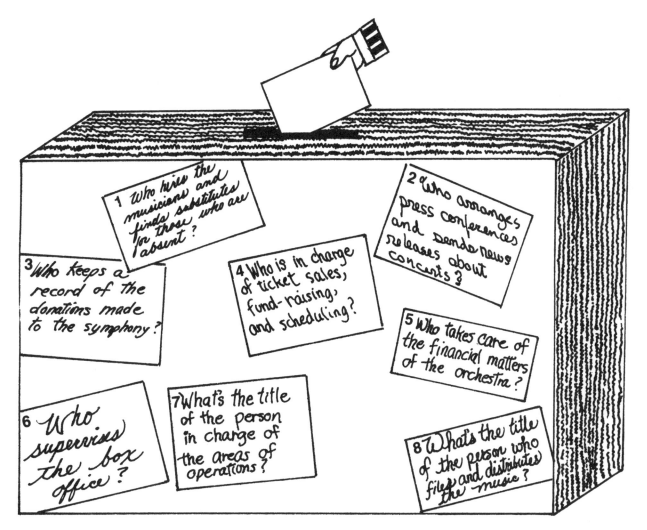

1 Who hires the musicians and finds substitutes for those who are absent?

2 Who arranges press conferences and sends news releases about concerts?

3 Who keeps a record of the donations made to the symphony?

4 Who is in charge of ticket sales, fund-raising, and scheduling?

5 Who takes care of the financial matters of the orchestra?

6 Who supervises the box office?

7 What's the title of the person in charge of the areas of operations?

8 What's the title of the person who files and distributes the music?

(In alphabetical order)

a. ____ Bookkeeper

b. ____ Chief Administrator

c. ____ Director of Development

d. ____ Director of Ticket Sales

e. ____ Librarian

f. ____ Manager

g. ____ Personnel Manager

h. ____ Public Relations Director

# Activities for
# ROLE PLAYING USING NOTE-READING SKILLS

## WRITE A NEW SCHOOL SONG

Pretend that you have been asked by the principal of your school to write the lyrics for a new school song. Use this familiar melody by Franz Schubert for your tune and write your lyrics underneath the staffs. Be sure to match the words with the right notes. If you use more than one verse, write the additional verse(s) at the bottom of the page.

_____
(Title of School Song)

Words by _____    Music by Franz Schubert

**TIGHT SQUEEZE**                                              **7–41**

The student who copied this song needs your help. As you can see, the notes are squeezed together and do not match the words. Recopy the song to match the words with the notes. The first measure is done for you.

**Swing Low, Sweet Chariot**

Spiritual

## TRANSCRIBE FOR BEETHOVEN                    7–42

Imagine that Beethoven is alive and well today. He has asked you to transcribe this familiar tune of his. Some of the dotted quarter notes in the song have been left out. You are to complete the song using the code below. The numbers represent the scale degrees. Draw in the correct notes with their dots.

**CODE:**

Key of E ♭

Scale     1     2     3     4     5     6     7     8
Degrees

**Symphony No. 3 (*Eroica*) E flat, Opus 55**

Ludwig van Beethoven

Name _____

Date _____

Score _____

Class _____

## MAKE A PROMOTIONAL VIDEO

7–43

Pretend that you are the head of a video production company. You have been offered a contract from your local school coach to promote your football team through a TV video. Your coach has made a special request. First, the melody for your "promo" must be from Mozart's 40th Symphony. Next, the video must last no longer than fifteen seconds. Your video must be convincing enough (that your team is the best) to convince the taxpayers to financially support your school sports program.

You are the director! First, write the lyrics for the tune underneath the staffs below. Write the words to match the notes. Then, dissect the lyrics of the song, word for word, to break it down into four individual scenes. Draw the four scenes in order in the blocks below. Write the numbers on the top of the staff of the first measure that matches each scene. Later, enlarge the scenes on individual sheets of paper or on a long roll of paper and make a cassette tape of your music to complete your video.

**Symphony No. 40 in G minor, K550**

Arranged by _____

Mozart

## MAKE A DEMO TAPE

A leading promoter has asked you for a demo tape of your latest recording using the melody of the song, "Bingo." Here's what you do. First, make up new words to the song, "Bingo," being careful to write the words under the staff to match the notes. Then, complete the arrangement by composing two additional instrumental parts. Choose two different percussion instruments and make up your own notation. For example, two measures using a triangle might read like this: |♩♪♪♪♪ |♪ ✗ ♪ ✗ |. Be sure to include a key. A key for the example would read as follows: ♪ = triangle; ✗ = rest. After you have finished the arrangement, plan to tape record your music using one or more vocalists and at least three instrumentalists.

_____
**(Name of Song)**
**To the tune of "Bingo"**

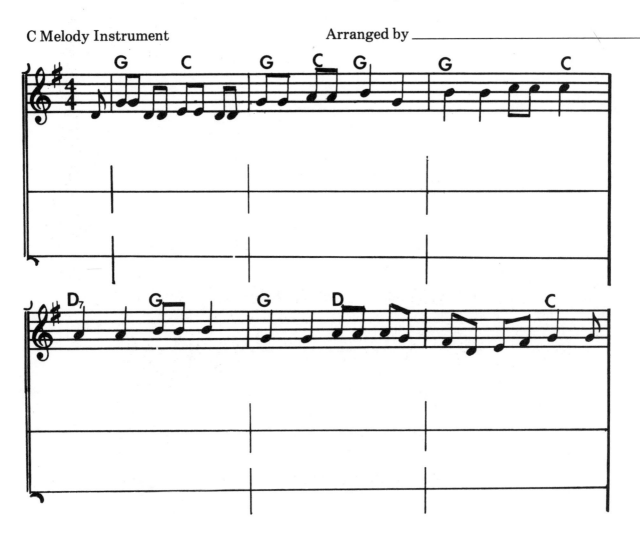

## PROGRAM THE COMPUTER

The computer transcribed Schumann's song in scale degrees instead of notes. You are to program the computer to print the song in quarter ( ♩♪ ) notes. Complete this task by drawing quarter notes on the staff to match the scale degrees above the staff.

( ⇓ = an octave lower)

## BE AN ORCHESTRATOR                                    7–46

One of the simplest forms in music is   A  B  A   form or three-part song form. In this form, the A sections are alike and the B section is different.

This piece is in   A  B  A   form. Tap out the rhythm to yourself. Then, draw a circle around the B section.

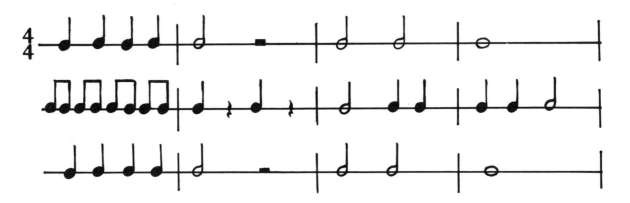

Now compose your own rhythm composition in   A  B  A   form. The meter signature and bar lines are drawn for you. Use four measures for each. The sections are labeled.

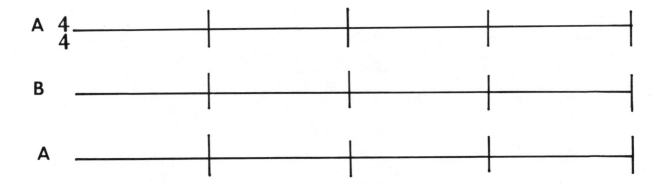

# WHAT'S THE TITLE?

7–47

Imagine that you are a music historian and
have been researching the composer Stephen
Foster. You have found the following songs of his, but the titles are missing. Listen to the
beginning lines of each to see how many you recognize. Then write the title under the tune. The
titles to choose from are:

"Old Black Joe"        "Beautiful Dreamer"        "Oh! Susanna"
"Some Folks Do"        "Old Folks at Home"        "My Old Kentucky Home"

1. _____

2. _____

3. _____

4. _____

5. _____

6. _____

# WRITE A JINGLE

7–48

Imagine that an advertising agency has asked you to write a jingle for a fifteen-second television commercial. Decide the name of the product, and who the consumer will be. Then write the melody and lyrics for your jingle using the staffs below.

Name of product: _____

Who will be the consumer? _____

## SWEET DREAM

Write a verse for a lullaby on the back of this page. Then rewrite the verse under the staff lines below as it would appear in a song book. Compose a melody to go with your verse. Notate it on the staff lines matching up each note and word.

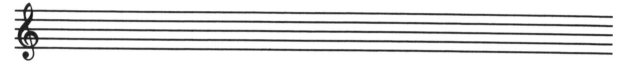

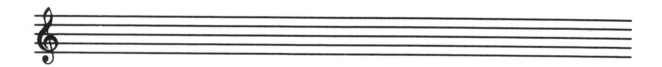

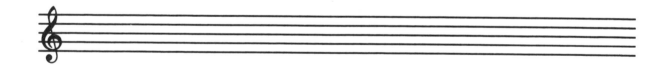

Name _____

Date _____

Score _____

Class _____

## TRANSPOSE IT FOR THE CLARINET 🎵

The school band will be playing "Beethoven's Tune" during its next concert. The music librarian can't find the part for the B♭ clarinet, so you've been asked to transpose the flute music for the clarinet. The music librarian has given you several clues in the following note to help you solve the problem.

Dear _____,

Thank you for volunteering to transpose this music. "Beethoven's Tune" is written in the Key of B♭ Major. It starts on the first scale degree. To rewrite this song for the B clarinet, the song must be written in the Key of C Major. (The B♭ clarinet sounds a Major second lower than what it is played.) To transpose the tune, first write the new Key Signature. Then write the same Time Signature as the flute part. Begin the song on the first scale degree of the new key and continue copying the song with each note a Major second higher than in the flute part.

Your grateful music librarian,

*Mrs. Clara Nett*

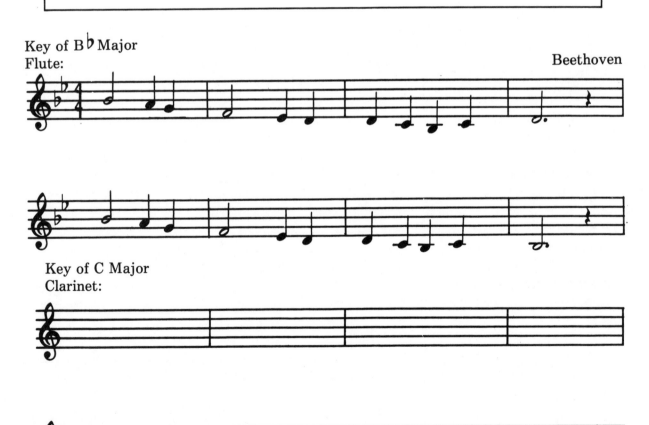

Key of B♭ Major
Flute:                                                                        Beethoven

Key of C Major
Clarinet:

# Answer Key
## for *Musicians in Action*

**7-1 DELIVER THE EXPRESS MAIL**

1. b
2. d
3. a.

4. f
5. e
6. c

**7-2 DISTRIBUTE THE MUSIC**

1. French horn
2. cello
3. violin
4. viola

5. harp
6. clarinet
7. flute
8. kettledrums

**7-3 INTERVIEW THE CONDUCTOR**

1. c
2. d
3. a

4. e
5. b

**7-4 THEY'RE REMEMBERED BY . . .**

The letter "A" has been placed between the composers' names and at the end.

1. Johann Sebastian Bach
2. George Frederick Handel
3. Ludwig van Beethoven
4. Frederic Chopin

5. Claude Debussy
6. Joseph Haydn
7. Wolfgang Amadeus Mozart
8. Richard Wagner

**7-5 WORK THE COMPUTER**

1. feedback
2. modulation
3. phonograph
4. transpose

5. notation
6. bluegrass
7. quartet
8. chorus

**7-6 BEST IN THE WORLD**

Answers will vary.

**7-7 SEE ME AT THE MET**

Answers will vary.

**7-8 CUSTOM MADE**

Answers will vary.

**7-9 SKETCH A SCENE**

Answers will vary.

**7-10  DESIGN YOUR SET**

Answers will vary.

**7-11  GUESS WHO**

Answers will vary.

**7-12  BE A STAGE MANAGER**

1. chair
2. bow

3. music stand
4. reed

**7-13  DELIVER THE GOODS**

1. strings
2. baton

3. staff paper
4. bugle

**7-14  LET'S GO SHOPPING**

Answers will vary.

**7-15  PRETEND YOU ARE THE MUSIC THERAPIST**

Answers will vary.

**7-16  BE A BIGWIG**

This activity is self-checking.

**7-17  QUESTIONNAIRE ABOUT THE CHURCH MUSICIAN**

Answers will vary.

**7-18  ASK THE RECRUITER**

Suggested questions are:

1. How do I qualify?
2. What positions are available?
3. How can I prepare for a career in the Armed Forces?
4. When are auditions held?
5. Do you have to devote your entire career to the service?
6. What are the benefits?

**7-19  REVIEW THE CRITIC**

Answers will vary.

**7-20  PLAN AHEAD**

Answers will vary.

**7-21  BE A PERSONNEL DIRECTOR**

Answers will vary.

**7-22  WRITE A RÉSUMÉ**

Answers will vary.

**7-23  GET THE JOB**

Answers will vary.

### 7-24  TOOLS OF THE TRADE

1. microphone
2. bow
3. beaters
4. baton
5. staff paper
6. tools
7. pick
8. mute

### 7-25  A VISIT WITH THE PRIVATE MUSIC TEACHER

1. schedule
2. job
3. studio
4. weekends
5. piano
6. organ
7. playing
8. best
9. teacher
10. improve

### 7-26  CLASSIFY THE STATIONS

Answers will vary.

### 7-27  WHOM SHOULD I CONTACT?

1. vocalist
2. accompanist
3. public relations director
4. composer
5. private teacher
6. arranger
7. editor
8. music teacher

### 7-28  FINISH THE CONSUMER GUIDE

Answers will vary.

### 7-29  CHECK THE CLASSIFIED

A person on a job search might use many sources to find a suitable position. It is important to note that many times there may be no ads in the classified section of the newspaper for a particular job. The following are only suggested answers:

1. 722-2801
   766-4555
2. 491-2390
3. 675-9723
   339-2121
4. 431-2806
5. 492-3660
6. 731-2828
   823-4568
   564-3890
7. 499-2834
   233-9457
8. 566-9781

### 7-30  COMPOSER CROSSWORD

This activity is self-checking.

### 7-31  LEARNING ABOUT LYRICISTS AND ARRANGERS

1. words
2. simple
3. lyrics
4. counts
5. dictionary
6. song
7. read
8. harmony
9. melody
10. clef

**7-32  A TUNER'S CHOICE**

| | | | |
|---|---|---|---|
| 1. | b | 6. | a |
| 2. | a | 7. | c |
| 3. | a | 8. | c |
| 4. | a | 9. | b |
| 5. | c | 10. | a |

**7-33  RIGHT ON TARGET**

This activity is self-checking. If correct, the answers will spell out I LOVE MUSIC starting from the bottom.

**7-34  CHECK YOUR SPELLING**

| | | | | | | | | |
|---|---|---|---|---|---|---|---|---|
| 1. | c | air | 5. | l | choir | 9. | k | pedal |
| 2. | i | aria | 6. | j | chorus | 10. | g | reed |
| 3. | f | bass | 7. | b | time | 11. | h | reel |
| 4. | a | beat | 8. | e | lyre | 12. | d | suite |

**7-35  PUTTING THE PIECES TOGETHER**

| | | | |
|---|---|---|---|
| 1. | WRITER | 7. | MANAGER OR PRODUCER |
| 2. | COMPOSER | 8. | INVESTOR |
| 3. | LYRICIST | 9. | PRESS AGENT |
| 4. | CONDUCTOR | 10. | STAGE MANAGER |
| 5. | SET DESIGNER | 11. | ACTOR |
| 6. | CHOREOGRAPHER | 12. | CRITIC |

The puzzle will spell out  RUN  FOR  THE  JOB.

**7-36  CALL ON US**

Answers will vary.

**7-37  COMPOSING A SONG**

1. F (The title is of great importance.)
2. T
3. F (Many performing artists write their own material today.)
4. T
5. T
6. T
7. F (Once a song is written, it is difficult to have it published.)
8. F (A composer should apply for a copyright on a song that he or she plans to publish.)

**7-38  BREAKING INTO POP**

| | | | | | | | |
|---|---|---|---|---|---|---|---|
| 1. | d | 3. | h | 5. | b | 7. | a |
| 2. | c | 4. | f | 6. | g | 8. | e |

"Code" letters in order from 1–8:

$$\frac{v}{1} \ \frac{o}{2} \ \frac{c}{3} \ \frac{a}{4} \ \frac{l}{5} \ \frac{i}{6} \ \frac{s}{7} \ \frac{t}{8}$$

**7–39 EMPTY THE QUESTION BOX**

a. 5
b. 4
c. 3
d. 6

e. 8
f. 7
g. 1
h. 2

**7–40 WRITE A NEW SCHOOL SONG**

Familiarize students with the melody of this song before attempting to complete the activity. Answers will vary.

**7–41 TIGHT SQUEEZE**

Sing and play this song prior to completing the activity.

**7–42 TRANSCRIBE FOR BEETHOVEN**

Review that a dot increases the value of a note by ½. A dot may be added to any kind of note to increase its value. Observe that the dot is added to the right of the note as in the examples. Notice also how the song begins on the upbeat where the initial note of the melody occurs before the first bar line. The remaining notes are in the last complete measure of the song.

This lesson was meant to be part of a listening or performing activity centered around Beethoven's Symphony No. 3 (*Eroica*).

**7–43 MAKE A PROMOTIONAL VIDEO**

This activity should be used in conjunction with listening to Mozart's 40th Symphony. Answers will vary.

**7–44 MAKE A DEMO TAPE**

Review "upbeat." The first note of the song occurs before the first bar line. The final beats of the first incomplete measure are found in the last measure of the song. Review the melody and words of "Bingo" prior to the activity. Answers will vary.

### 7-45  PROGRAM THE COMPUTER

Allow students to perform "A Little Piece" on a melody instrument upon completion of this activity.

Schumann

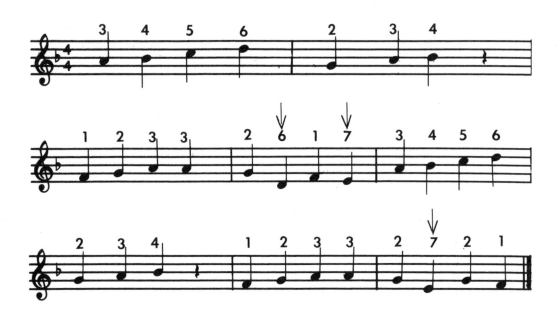

### 7-46  BE AN ORCHESTRATOR

Perform the example of  A  B  A  form prior to completing this activity. Use percussion instruments, melody instruments (using one note), sing on a syllable, and/or tap, clap, or snap the beats.

Have students perform their finished compositions individually. During another lesson, combine two or more rhythm compositions at the same time to listen how different orchestrations sound together.

### 7-47  WHAT'S THE TITLE?

Include information about Stephen Foster in this activity and familiarize students with the music in the activity prior to the lesson. There are many resource books available, including the encyclopedia, for the students to find out more about this composer and his music.

1. "My Old Kentucky Home"
2. "Some Folks Do"
3. "Oh! Susanna"
4. "Old Folks at Home"
5. "Old Black Joe"
6. "Beautiful Dreamer"

### 7-48  WRITE A JINGLE

A jingle writer must consider not only the company, the product, and the market to be reached, but also the form of music, the style, and the orchestration. For beginners in note-reading, this lesson might well be completed as a group project. First, write the lyrics and melody on the chalkboard or overhead projector. More advanced students might help notate the melody while others copy it on their activity sheet. Two or three ideas might be gathered for each phrase. Then ask students to vote for the one they like best. After completing the activity, encourage students to make a video as explained in the activity "Make a Promotional Video." Allow students to perform their jingles also.

### 7–49  SWEET DREAMS

This activity might be done as a group project. While one person writes the lyrics and notation on the chalkboard, the others could copy the song on their activity sheets. For more advanced students, you might allow them to create their own melody and verse.

### 7–50  TRANSPOSE IT FOR THE CLARINET

Incorporate "Beethoven's Tune" as a listening and/or performing activity with this lesson.

Clarinet:                                                                                           Beethoven

# Progress Chart for
## *Musicians in Action*

Use this chart to keep a record of activities completed for each class. List your classes (or students) in the given spaces at the right. As each activity is completed for a class, mark an "X" in the appropriate column.

**Activity Number/Title**　　　　　　**Skill Involved**

### Role Playing in the World of Work

| | | |
|---|---|---|
| 7-1 | DELIVER THE EXPRESS MAIL | Drawing an item to match the job title |
| 7-2 | DISTRIBUTE THE MUSIC (Music Librarian) | Matching the name to the instrument |
| 7-3 | INTERVIEW THE CONDUCTOR (Conductor) | Matching interview questions with answers |
| 7-4 | THEY'RE REMEMBERED BY . . . (Historian) | Decoding names of famous composers and determining how they are remembered |
| 7-5 | WORK THE COMPUTER (Computer Programmer) | Answering general composition questions using a syllabic computer |

### Role Playing Through Creative Drawing

| | | |
|---|---|---|
| 7-6 | BEST IN THE WORLD | Drawing an instrumentalist or vocalist performing a favorite type of music |
| 7-7 | SEE ME AT THE MET (Opera Star) | Drawing oneself on stage at the Metropolitan Opera House |
| 7-8 | CUSTOM MADE (Instrumentalist) | Drawing two musicians ready to perform for two different events |
| 7-9 | SKETCH A SCENE (Scene Designer) | Drawing a scene from a favorite musical |
| 7-10 | DESIGN YOUR SET (Set Designer) | Creating a set for a favorite production |
| 7-11 | GUESS WHO | Choosing a person for outstanding music achievement and illustrating the person |

| Activity Number/Title | Skill Involved |
|---|---|

| | | |
|---|---|---|

**7-12    BE A STAGE MANAGER** (Stage Manager)
Drawing items to be delivered to orchestra members

**7-13    DELIVER THE GOODS**
Finishing pictures to show people using items from the music store

## Role Playing Through Creative Writing

**7-14    LET'S GO SHOPPING**
Selecting an item from a music store, explaining its use and related career

**7-15    PRETEND YOU ARE THE MUSIC THERAPIST** (Music Therapist)
Making simple lesson plan for children with special learning problems

**7-16    BE A BIGWIG** (Music Representative)
Providing guidance to aspiring musicians

**7-17    QUESTIONNAIRE ABOUT THE CHURCH MUSICIAN** (Church Musician)
Answering questions about the responsibilities of the church musician

**7-18    ASK THE RECRUITER** (Military Musician)
Writing questions to fit answers about music opportunities in the Armed Forces

**7-19    REVIEW THE CRITIC** (Music Critic)
Reading an article by a music critic and answering questions about it

**7-20    PLAN AHEAD** (Music Intern)
Planning a lesson to teach the music class

**7-21    BE A PERSONNEL DIRECTOR** (Personnel Director)
Writing a job description for a position in the music industry

**7-22    WRITE A RÉSUMÉ**
Writing a résumé for employment in the field of music

**7-23    GET THE JOB**
Writing a letter of application for a job in the field of music

## Exploring Music-Related Jobs Through Problem-Solving Experiences

**7-24    TOOLS OF THE TRADE**
Matching the tool with the job title

| Activity Number/Title | | Skill Involved | | | | |
|---|---|---|---|---|---|---|
| 7-25 | A VISIT WITH THE PRIVATE MUSIC TEACHER (Private Music Teacher) | Using a notation code to finish a story about the private music teacher | | | | |
| 7-26 | CLASSIFY THE STATIONS | Listing radio stations by name, location on the dial, and type of music | | | | |
| 7-27 | WHOM SHOULD I CONTACT? | Naming the occupation to match the description | | | | |
| 7-28 | FINISH THE CONSUMER GUIDE | Writing where in town a person would purchase music goods or services | | | | |
| 7-29 | CHECK THE CLASSIFIED | Reading ads to decide where to call for certain music-related jobs | | | | |
| 7-30 | COMPOSER CROSSWORD | Using words from the puzzle to complete statements about composers | | | | |
| 7-31 | LEARNING ABOUT LYRICISTS AND ARRANGERS (Lyricist and Arranger) | Using letters from the keyboard to complete sentences about the lyricist and arranger | | | | |
| 7-32 | A TUNER'S CHOICE (Piano Tuner) | Completing sentences about the piano tuner using multiple choice | | | | |
| 7-33 | RIGHT ON TARGET | Matching general music career-related questions with answers | | | | |
| 7-34 | CHECK YOUR SPELLING (Music Librarian) | Using the dictionary to match music words with their definitions | | | | |
| 7-35 | PUTTING THE PIECES TOGETHER | Matching jobs and descriptions relating to producing a musical | | | | |
| 7-36 | CALL ON US | Listing people in the community to call for music-related questions | | | | |
| 7-37 | COMPOSING A SONG (Composer) | Answering true/false statements about the composers | | | | |
| 7-38 | BREAKING INTO POP (Pop Musician) | Matching questions with answers about becoming a pop musician | | | | |

| Activity Number/Title | Skill Involved | |
|---|---|---|
| | | 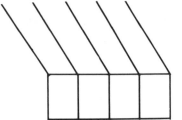 |
| 7-39 EMPTY THE QUESTION BOX (Symphony Administrator) | Matching jobs in the symphony with their descriptions | |

**Role Playing Using Note-Reading Skills**

| 7-40 WRITE A NEW SCHOOL SONG (Lyricist) | Writing lyrics for a new school song |
|---|---|
| 7-41 TIGHT SQUEEZE (Transcriber) | Rewriting a song using better spacing than that in the example |
| 7-42 TRANSCRIBE FOR BEETHOVEN (Transcriber) | Using dotted quarter notes listed to complete the theme for *Eroica* |
| 7-43 MAKE A PROMOTIONAL VIDEO (Songwriter) | Creating lyrics to the tune of Mozart's 40th and drawing four scenes for a football promo |
| 7-44 MAKE A DEMO TAPE (Orchestrator) | Creating two percussion scores to accompany the song "Bingo" |
| 7-45 PROGRAM THE COMPUTER (Computer Programmer) | Drawing quarter notes in the key of F Major to complete a tune by Schumann |
| 7-46 BE AN ORCHESTRATOR (Orchestrator) | Composing an original rhythmic composition in ABA form |
| 7-47 WHAT'S THE TITLE? (Music Historian) | Recognizing beginning lines of Stephen Foster songs by listening to the melodies |
| 7-48 WRITE A JINGLE (Songwriter) | Composing a melody and lyrics for a television commercial |
| 7-49 SWEET DREAMS (Composer) | Writing a verse for a lullaby and composing a melody to accompany it |
| 7-50 TRANSPOSE IT FOR THE CLARINET (Arranger) | Transposing a simple tune from the Key of B-flat Major to C Major |

© 1987 by Parker Publishing Company, Inc.

# Musicians in Action

accompanist

arranger

church musician

choreographer

composer

computer programmer

conductor

historian

instrumentalist

jingle writer

lyricist

music critic

music editor

music historian

music intern

music instructor (teacher)

music profession

music publisher

music technician

music therapist

musician

orchestrator

performer

piano tuner

pop musician

private teacher

recording artist

scene designer

set designer

songwriter

stage manager

symphony administrator

transcriber

vocalist

Name _____

Date _____

# Craft Project
# for *Musicians in Action*

## BADGE DESIGNING CONTEST

**Objective:** The badges will help promote music education by communicating to the community the value of music in the curriculum. This activity is appropriate for "Music In Our Schools" Week.

**Materials Needed:**

- Copies of the badge forms
- Marker
- Scissors

**Construction Directions:**

1. Use the frames to communicate the idea that music is valuable in your school. Design several different badges or perfect one particular idea. Learn by doing and experiment! Use your imagination to create an original idea. Keep in mind that your badge will be used during a campaign to promote music education during "Music In Our Schools" Week.

2. When you are finished, cut out your badge and write your name on the back.

3. Here are sample badges to show you what can be done. Do not use any of these ideas for your own design.

**Uses:**

1. Design a box for the students to drop in their designs and encourage students to submit several different ideas.

2. Start early in the school year and find out what the theme of "Music In Our Schools" Week is for this year's promotion. Encourage students to design their badges using that theme.

3. Choose a panel of judges to select the best badge from all the entries. Consider faculty members, community leaders, politicians, and/or school board members for this panel.

4. Make it an all-out campaign. After the badge has been chosen as the winning entry, award the artist. Present the award during a special event, an assembly program, or a special "Music In Our Schools" Week presentation. Use the winning badge design in the following way or in a way adaptable to your teaching situation.

   a. Copy the badge design on a set of black frames ready to duplicate. Run off as many copies as you need for your students' uses.

   b. Distribute the badges to the students as they sign for the number received.

   c. Provide each student with a sheet of paper ready-to-go or have students write the theme for the "Music In Our Schools" Week at the top or write "I Support Music In Our Schools." The students will be taking a poll with the sheet.

   d. Have the students canvass their neighborhoods. With the poll sheet and badges in hand, have students ask their families, friends, and neighbors to wear the badge for the week (or for one particular day during the "Music In Our Schools" Week) and ask the individuals to write their signatures on the poll if they support music in our schools. Students should be prepared to answer why music is necessary and important in the curriculum. Be sure the canvassing is done the week or day prior to "Music In Our Schools" Week. As an incentive, award the student who distributes the most badges.

e. Provide the entire school staff, faculty, and students with badges to wear during "Music In Our Schools" Week.

f. Make a bulletin board display for your classroom (preferably for open house) with the theme "We Support Music In Our Schools." Exhibit the poll sheets and all the badges that were entered in the judging.

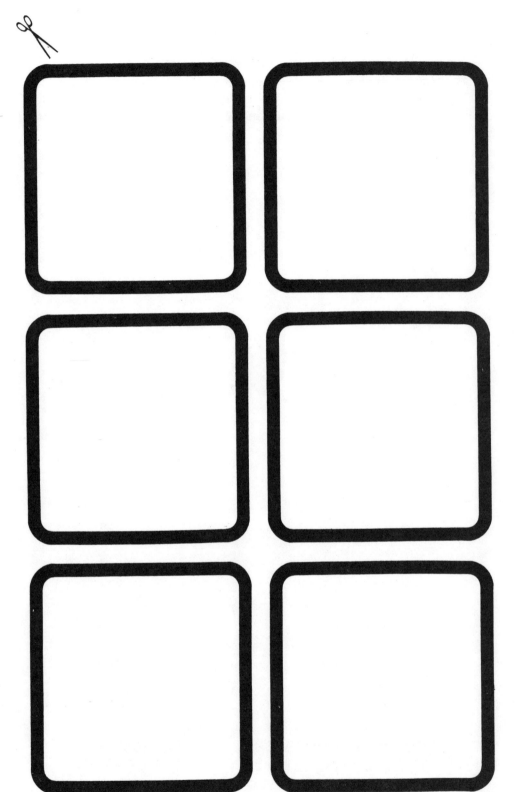

# Incentive Badges

*To the teacher:* Cut apart badges and keep in a handy 3″ × 5″ file box along with tape. Encourage students to write their names and the date on the backs of their badges and to wear them.

A Pledge

DO IT NOW!

_____

_____

(name)

MUSIC TOKEN

MUSIC          AWARD

THANKS

BEST BEHAVIOR

"Busy as a bee"

MUSIC AWARD

CERTIFICATE

TO:          FOR:

**DOUBLE EXTRA BONUS**

MUSIC AWARD

NAME _____

_____

_____

WITH THIS COUPON...

NAME _____

IS ENTITLED TO _____

_____

MUSIC AWARD

For hopping to it!
Good helper badge
in music class.

Watch OUT!

Best in the class . . . .
MUSIC AWARD

**Creative WRITING**

MUSIC CLASS AWARD

**Great News**

best     work

MUSIC AWARD

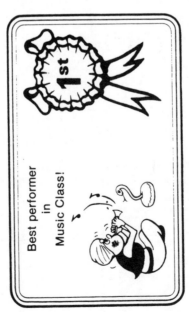

#

DOG GONE GOOD
MUSIC AWARD!

(name)

**WELCOME**

to
MUSIC CLASS

Congratulations!

creative drawing
MUSIC AWARD

1st

Best performer
in
Music Class!

DON'T FORGET!

MUSIC

# MUSIC SHARE-A-GRAM

TO: _____ DATE _____
        (Parent's Name)

FROM: _____ SCHOOL _____
        (Classroom Music Teacher)

RE: _____ CLASS _____
        (Student's Name)

To help you recognize your child's success in music class or any area that needs attention the following observation(s) has/have been made.

| | Exceptional | Satisfactory | Unsatisfactory |
|---|---|---|---|
| Shows musical aptitude | | | |
| Shows creativity | | | |
| Shows talent | | | |
| Shows initiative | | | |
| Self-concept in music class | | | |
| Fairness in dealing with classmates | | | |
| Self-direction | | | |
| Care of instrument and equipment | | | |
| Reaction to constructive criticism | | | |
| Observes music class rules | | | |
| Starts and completes work on time | | | |
| Generally follows directions | | | |

over for comments ▶

---

# RETURN-A-GRAM

TO: _____ DATE _____
        (Classroom Music Teacher)

FROM: _____ SCHOOL _____
        (Parent's Name)

RE: _____ CLASS _____
        (Student's Name)

Please write your comments or questions on the back and return. If you want to be called for a parent-teacher conference, indicate below.

# STUDENT RECORD PROFILE CHART

_____ Class _____ Year _____

(Student's Name)

Select the appropriate data in parentheses for each category, i, ii, iii, and iv, and record the information in the chart below as shown in the example.

i.—Unit Number for _Music Curriculum Activities Library_ (1, 2, 3, 4, 5, 6, 7)

ii.—Date (Day/Month)

iii.—Semester (1, 2, 3, 4) or Summer School: Session 1 (S1), Session 2 (S2)

iv.—Score: Select one of the three grading systems, a., b., or c., that applies to the specific activity.

a.

| | |
|---|---|
| (O) | = Outstanding |
| (G) | = Good |
| (S) | = Satisfactory |
| (NI) | = Needs Improvement |
| (U) | = Unsatisfactory |
| (I) | = Incomplete |
| (—) | = Absent |

b.

| | |
|---|---|
| (A) | = 93–100 [percentage score] |
| (B) | = 85–92 |
| (C) | = 75–84 |
| (D) | = 70–74 |
| (F) | = 0–69 |
| (I) | = Incomplete |
| (—) | = Absent |

c.

| | |
|---|---|
| (R/P): | |
| R | = Correct number of responses. |
| P | = Possible correct number of responses. |
| (I) | = Incomplete |
| (—) | = Absent |

| i | ii |
|---|---|
| iii | iv |

Student's Name _____ Class _____ Year _____

# MUSIC SELF-IMPROVEMENT CHART (for student use)

a. On the back of this chart write your goal(s) for music class at the beginning of each semester.
b. On a separate sheet record the date and each new music skill you have acquired during the semester.

c. MUSIC SHARE-A-GRAM (date sent to parent)

d. RETURN-A-GRAM (date returned to teacher)

e. MUSIC AWARD BADGES (date and type rec'd)

1.
2.
3.

f. SPECIAL MUSIC RECOGNITION (date and type rec'd)

1.
2.
3.

g. SPECIAL MUSIC EVENT ATTENDANCE RECORD (date and name of special performance, recital, rehearsal, concert, field trip, film, workshop, seminar, institute, etc.)

1.
2.
3.
4.

h. ABOVE AND BEYOND: Extra Credit Projects (date and name of book report, classroom performance, construction of hand-made instrument, report on special music performance on TV, etc.)

1.
2.
3.
4.

i. PROGRESS REPORT/REPORT CARD RECORD (semester and grade received)

1.
2.
3.
4.

j. MUSIC SIGN-OUT RECORD (name of instrument, music, book or equipment with sign-out date and due date)

1.
2.
3.
4.
5.
6.
7.
8.
9.
10.